D0777709

# Virtual Reality for Beginners!

How to Understand, Use & Create with VR

1st Edition

# By Murray Ramirez

JAN -- 2017

Bullard Sanford
Memorial Library
320 W Huron Ave. Vassar, MI

**Copyright 2016 by Murray Ramirez - All rights reserved.**

This document is geared towards providing exact and reliable information in regards to the topic and issue covered. The publication is sold with the idea that the publisher is not required to render accounting, officially permitted, or otherwise, qualified services. If advice is necessary, legal or professional, a practiced individual in the profession should be ordered.

- From a Declaration of Principles which was accepted and approved equally by a Committee of the American Bar Association and a Committee of Publishers and Associations.

In no way is it legal to reproduce, duplicate, or transmit any part of this document in either electronic means or in printed format. Recording of this publication is strictly prohibited and any storage of this document is not allowed unless with written permission from the publisher. All rights reserved.

The information provided herein is stated to be truthful and consistent, in that any liability, in terms of inattention or otherwise, by any usage or abuse of any policies, processes, or directions contained within is the solitary and utter responsibility of the recipient reader. Under no

circumstances will any legal responsibility or blame be held against the publisher for any reparation, damages, or monetary loss due to the information herein, either directly or indirectly.

Respective authors own all copyrights not held by the publisher.

The information herein is offered for informational purposes solely, and is universal as so. The presentation of the information is without contract or any type of guarantee assurance.

The trademarks that are used are without any consent, and the publication of the trademark is without permission or backing by the trademark owner. All trademarks and brands within this book are for clarifying purposes only and are the owned by the owners themselves, not affiliated with this document.

# Table of Contents

# Introduction

Virtual reality (VR) devices and machines were already present long before the 90s. The early designs were bulky and goofy, and most of them fell short of what we were expecting. They might not be much but their presence always made us feel like futuristic technology was just around the corner.

Then the 21st century arrived and yet, none of them still delivered. None of them were nothing like what we read in sci-fi books from the 30s and 50s.

Decades after the 60s, when the first VR machine was built, ensuing virtual reality technology sparked interest not only within the computing world, but within the public as well. They all failed however. That is, until 2016 came along. Breakthrough systems debuted. Finally, sci-fi-quality VR devices started to emerge.

While head-mounted displays (HMD) failed in the past, VRs today offer virtual experiences that can literally bring users to new heights. Users can travel space, live out a concert on stage, and scale the wall of the Rocky Mountains. No more heavily-pixelated graphics, slow-moving scenes, and weighty headsets. Users are no longer just playing. Users are now transported to new "experiences."

VR enables users to experience different virtual environments by making the brain think that the user is somewhere else. It's literally tricking us. It allows people to explore and interact with virtual simulations. It does so by combining high-level graphics, position tracking, and motion-sensors. To make experiences more realistic, developers added photogrammetry which captures surfaces and textures making objects seem truly lifelike.

However, VR is not all about virtual experiences in games. Various industries are eyeing new VR developments for its potential to enhance movies, education, other technologies, and training in the military and medical fields.

In Europe, medical residents were able to view an operation as if they were doing it themselves. A surgeon who performed the operation live-streamed the process in 360-degree video. The students received the video feed through headsets that were provided for them.

Meanwhile in the US, VR is already being used in many forms. The Department of Defense tested VR as therapy for Post-Traumatic Stress Disorder (PTSD) widespread among soldiers.

The website YouVisit enables people to explore the world through virtual videos shared by its users. The studio Virtual Reality Company is creating a movie that will allow viewers to experience VR through headsets.

VR can change our lives dramatically. However, concerns and challenges are unavoidable. Researchers believe that long-term use and exposure to VR can affect human brains negatively. At the same time, they doubt that VR will ever improve our way of thinking or how the world works.

In truth, the scientific community as a whole is divided on the topic. Mark Zuckerberg, Facebook co-founder, on the biggest social media network's $2 billion purchase of Oculus Rift (the latest in VR device and technology) said that through VR, they will enable its users "to experience the impossible."

I want to thank you and congratulate you for downloading the e-Book, *"Virtual Reality for Beginners! How to Understand, Use and Create with VR"*

Together, let's learn how virtual reality started and how it is shaping the world today. This e-Book contains information on how you can use VR and benefit from it. I'll show how to create a

VR, develop with it, and configure your hardware systems, so they can be VR-friendly.

This book will also help you to decide and choose whether to get a VR device or not – only the latest and best VR reviews are featured in this e-Book.

Thanks again for purchasing this book. I hope you enjoy it!

# Chapter 1 – Virtual Reality Defined

While virtual reality is essentially rooted in science and technology, its concept and the words themselves took its form in the art and literary world.

Antonin Artaud, one of the most influential French theater directors of the 20th century, observed how characters and objects were like an illusion in a theater play. They were in fact, unreal and yet, there they were – moving, within reach of an audience.

In Artaud's collection of essays released in 1938, he called the illusionary characters and objects, "la realite virtuelle." It wasn't until an English translation of his essays that were published 20 years later, that the words "virtual reality" was first seen and read.

A year later in 1959, scientists began using the word "virtual" to describe computer memory that appeared real and true, although they didn't physically exist. It was the first incidence of the words "virtual reality" being used in relation to technology. Today that would be the RAM (random access memory) and ROM (read-only memory).

However, according to a 1987 article cited by the Oxford English Dictionary entitled "Virtual Reality," the word "virtual" has been in use since the mid-1400s. Back then, the word was used to describe something that can produce an effect that is neither true nor factual.

In the 1970s, Myron Krueger, one of the pioneers of VR, first used the term "artificial reality" to describe his early interactive works. Further advancements in technology led to the increase in sci-fi movies and books being released. This created a sudden interest in virtual reality and anything related to science and technology.

However, it wasn't until the late 1980s when VR became popular and widely accepted, especially in the United States. Allan Metcalf and David Barnhart, authors of "America in So Many Words: Words That Have Shaped America" published in 1997, mentioned in their book that computer geeks in the 80s started creating their own virtual reality, confined in an electronic space. It was during this time that scientists were able to produce the first "virtual glove," which will be discussed in detail later.

Since then, VR has been used synonymous to computer-simulated reality, artificial reality, or immersive multimedia.

Some technologies compare VR with augmented reality (AR). Initially, the two share similar elements. AR incorporates computer-generated content in the virtual scene it produces. VR doesn't. However, in today's technology, it's common to see and experience the two .

Knowing all this would leave one last question. What is virtual reality really? How does it work? Is it important? Would it affect me and you in today's world?

Well, let's find out.

# What is Virtual Reality?

According to the Merriam-Webster Dictionary, virtual reality is

*"a sensory stimuli (as sounds and sights) experienced in an artificial environment provided by a computer. It is the technology used to create or access a virtual reality in which one's actions determine what partially happens in the virtual environment."*

Meanwhile, Encyclopedia Britannica defines VR as

*"the use of computer simulation and modeling enabling a person to interact with a sensory and three-dimensional (3D) visual environment that is artificial."*

Typically, virtual reality is used to describe computer technologies that create realistic, imaginary settings that VR users see and feel.

A "real" environment is reproduced through computer technologies that use software. It generates images and sounds, and sometimes, other sensory effects. Outside sound and sceneries are cut off, so users can focus on what they can see in the virtual world.

Users can interact with the imaginary environment they see using a combination of various VR devices, which in effect, stimulates physical presence.

VR devices enable users to look around the virtual environment that they are in. In some cases, it can even replicate sensory experiences such as touch and smell. It can provide this physical presence through VR screens or goggles.

VR screens today come in different forms. Projector screens and computer monitors are the most commonly used VR screens. However, VR headsets, or HMDs are increasingly becoming more popular nowadays.

*Example of VR used in other applications. Here, VR is used in combat training by the Netherlands Army at the 7th US Army Joint Multinational Training Command. (c) Road to VR*

VR today is used in various applications. It is widely used as a game device, but its advance technology (haptic systems) opened a way for other industries to see its potential. Training in the medical field, military, and aerospace use VR because of its tactile information capability, which is part of the advancement in haptic systems. This, along with the other advancement that VR provides, will be discussed further later.

Aside from VR screens, VR also use input devices that can transmit sensations and vibrations. This creates a lifelike experience in a remote-communication environment, often supporting ideas of telepresence and virtual artifact. Common input devices include mouse, keyboard, various game controllers, treadmill or platform, and wired gloves.

## VR through Time

While the words "virtual reality" were only officially used in the 1980s to name its field, its history dates way back. Before 19th century ended and the 20th started, a few notable VR-similar devices were developed.

### 1800s

In 1838, a Victorian era British physicist named Charles Wheatsone invented the stereoscope (although he was more popular for his invention of the Wheatstone bridge, a laboratory device). It was a goggle-like device that enables a viewer to see pictures in three dimensions. Primitive as it was, it is still used today (as his Wheatstone bridge is) in aerial photographs and x-rays.

More than ten years later in 1849, a Scottish physicist by the name of David Brewster (Father of modern experimental optics) improved Wheatstone's work and called it a lenticular stereoscope. He also invented the kaleidoscope in 1815, but his improved version of the stereoscope sealed his contribution in the field of optics.

**1920s-1930s**

It took more than fifty years before any improvement in virtual reality was seen. In 1929, the Link Trainer was invented. Edward Link, an American aviator, was the one who created it.

Although self-taught in aviation, his experience while training to fly aircrafts convinced him to come up with a way to help others to learn. Link's work is considered as the first successful flight simulator to be used in the military. Two others came before his work, but proved to be risky. There were no computers involved, but the lifelike cockpit scenarios he created help trained pilots which proved to be helpful during World War II.

In the 1930s, the concept of a goggle being used as a VR device entered the scene. Stanley G. Weinbaum, an American sci-fi writer, mentioned a VR-like device called Pygmalion's Spectacles in his book with the same name (published 1935). According to him, the spectacle's wearer could experience an imaginary world that seemed real, complete with images, sounds, and smell. Because of this, many VR enthusiasts believed Weinbaum as a visionary in the field of VR.

**1950s-1970s**

The first working VR machine was invented in 1957 by Morton Heilig, an American cinematographer. He called his machine the Sensorama. His machine included an arcade-type box with a seat where viewers can watch moving, virtual scenes. It would've been successful if not for the expensive costs of filming the virtual sceneries.

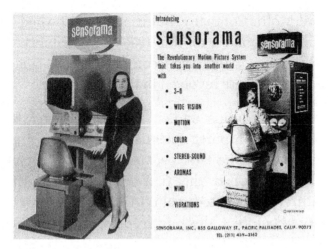

*Marketing peripherals for Heilig's Sensorama.*
*(c) Morton Heilig*

A few years later in 1960, Heilig next invented the Telesphere Mask, a stereoscopic head-mounted display, which was considered to be the first of its kind to be actually built. There were many others before it. Some were patented and some were not, but none were built.

Heilig's mask was the first HMD that provided 3D, wide vision and stereo sound. However, it didn't have any motion tracking capabilities just like the others that weren't built at all.

A year later, Headsight was introduced to the world. It was created by James Bryan and Charles Comeau, American engineers working for the Philco Corporation (then a subsidiary of

Ford Motor Company, but is currently owned by Philips). It had a motion tracking capability on each lens. Still, no computers or image generation were involved in the experience.

Before the 1960s ended, Ivan Sutherland (an American computer scientist) and Bob Sproull (his student who later became director of Oracle Labs) developed the first HMD system that featured augmented reality. Unlike other HMDs created before it, this one used a helmet attached to a periscope-like device. The appearance of the periscope attached to a ceiling gave its name the Sword of Damocles.

During the same year in 1968, the first flight simulator to be built with a visual display system was developed by Thomas Furness, an American engineer. His work became the trademark program for the Super Cockpit flight simulator system fully implemented in the 1980s. It was a significant improvement in the development of VR, AR, and flight simulator systems of that time.

In 1969, Krueger finally entered the scene. His introduction of "artificial reality" was ahead of his time. It consisted of a combination of interactive art and VR. He released a series of his work which were later collectively named Videoplace technology. It involved computer-generated virtual environments that allowed people to communicate with each other.

**1980s-1990s**

Finally it was in the 1980s that the name "virtual reality" was given as a name to this field. It was also within these decades that the masses became familiar with VR.

The year was 1987. Jason Lanier, a computer scientist, and some of his acquaintances built VR devices and sold them through Lanier's company, the Visual Programming Lab (VPL). The company introduced the Eyephone and the Dataglove (together with Tom Zimmerman, a former colleague from Atari), the first VR devices to be sold commercially. Other companies followed soon.

In 1991, the first game-oriented VR machines were released to the market. Because VR was new to the public, it easily became popular. By the following year, the first VR movie was shown in theaters in the US (and some parts of the world) – The Lawnmower Man.

Based in part to Lanier's work, The Lawnmower Man allowed VR to reach a wider audience. There was one other VR film released in 1983, the Brainstorm. However, the death of one of its main characters (Natalie Wood) in between filming made it an unpopular film.

After the success of The Lawnmower Man, VR devices for games started to enter the market.

*The Lawnmower Man (1992) is a movie about virtual reality and is loosely based on Jason Lanier's VPL research. It stars Pierce Brosnan and Jeff Fahey, and directed by Brett Leonard. (c) Wikipedia*

It was Sega that first introduced VR headsets for its Sega Genesis game console. The company's HMD, sold in 1993, appeared futuristic compared to early prototypes of VR. It was worn as a visor with a small LCD screen in replacement of glasses.

Two years later in 1995, rival Nintendo also released its own version, the Virtual Boy. Unlike Sega's HMD, this one can produce 3D graphics and was way cheaper.

Unfortunately, software support was still not fully developed during those years. This prompted the first VRs to be discontinued not long after.

Interest in VR gained momentum again with the showing of the movie series, the Matrix, starting in 1999. Neo, the movie's protagonist, lived in a fully simulated VR world in which he has to escape from. The movie's success caused a major socio-cultural impact the world over.

## 2000s

The beginning of the 21st century saw major improvements in the field of VR. Many more VR headsets were developed for games. More importantly, various industries recognized VR as a useful tool in advancing their trade.

Advancements in VR positively continued for the next 15 years. Here are some of them:

* *Mobile technology has opened up new VR possibilities*

* *Smartphones enabled anyone to experience VR and to have    practical, lightweight VR devices of their own*

* *Smartphones now have 3D graphics and high-density displays*

* *VR-based video games are on the rise and it continues to tap the interest of many with VR. This drives consumer-based needs to develop new VRs.*

* *Computers today have capabilities that can detect and control virtual movements, sense movements using cameras, and recognize human interfaces.*

Here is a quick timeline of major developments in VR over the years leading to the present.

**2010**

Google introduced stereoscopic 3D mode in the Street View of Google Maps

**2010**

Palmer Luckey developed the first Oculus Rift prototype

**2013**

Nintendo filed a patent for 3D effect and technology in 2D television

**2013**

Vendetta Online, a game developed by Guild Software, became the first game that can be played with the Occulus Rift

**2013**

Many other VR devices similar to Oculus entered the consumer market

**2014**

Facebook Inc. purchased Oculus VR, the company established by Luckey which produces his VR headset, Oculus Rift

## 2014

Sony announced the Project Morpheus, a codename used for the Playstation VR, a headset for the PlayStation 4 game console.

## 2014

Google announced the development of a simpler VR prototype, the Google Cardboard. It can use smartphones as VR devices.

## 2015

HTC announced it was developing a VR headset together with its partner, Valve Corporation.

## 2016

Facebook, Google, Sony, and HTC releases their own VR devices.

## Present

The release of VR devices by major players in 2016 has dubbed the year as the "Year of Virtual Reality."

With all the hype, let's see what the fuss all about is with VR by knowing what it can do.

# Chapter 2 – Getting Started

To better understand virtual reality, let's start with the basics.

## The Science of VR

How does VR work? Let's look at the recent developments in this field to get an explanation on how they work.

## The CAVE

CAVE is recursive acronym for Cave Automatic Virtual Environment. It is the virtual world in which VR users are immersed in. It is shaped like a cube wherein VR users stand in the middle, attached to HMDs or VR goggles and surrounded by various VR tracking technologies. Here is where the "magic" happens.

Projectors feed images onto the walls of the cubed CAVE. VR users wear HMDs or VR goggles which enables them to see 3D images using the process of stereoscopy. Three dimensional images seen in CAVEs are generated by powerful computers, while user's movements are captured by motion capture systems. Movements are then displayed for users to see through their HMDs or VR goggles.

## CAVE Interaction

The aim with VR systems is divided into two major goals. One is to provide an experience of total virtual immersion. A user should be totally immersed that the surroundings, the attached headset and accessories themselves, and even the physical world itself are all forgotten.

Two is that VR systems should be able to create life size, 3D, 360-degree virtual environment that are not held by boundaries associated with television or computer screens. Unlike AR which superimposes images onto the view of the real world, VR world is 100% manufactured.

In a CAVE system, interaction is key. When this is combined with total immersion, it is called "Telepresence."

In telepresence, VR users can interact with the virtual world around them and be totally immersed in it. For this to completely happen, VR input devices are needed.

### Physical Components

The latest VRs today come in HMD or goggle forms. Considering this, there are four important hardware components (physical components) in VR devices:

1   A computer

2   A console to run the game or smartphone to run the app

3   A headset or smartphone for the display in front of your eyes

4   An input device (one or more) – for example: controllers, head tracking, hand tracking, voice recorder, and trackpads or on-device buttons

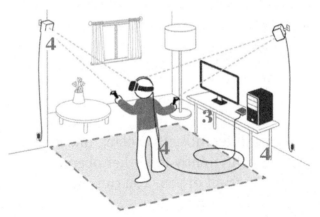

Seen here is a standard VR system setup called the CAVE. There are different setups of CAVE

systems, but home setups like this this one is the most basic kind.

Videos and images are sent from the computer or console to the HMD using an HDMI cable. In other forms of HMDs using smartphones, no HMDI cables are involved. The smartphone itself sends videos and images to the HMD.

From the HDMI cable, images and video feeds are sent to one LCD display per eye. In other HMDs, especially in older versions, there are lenses in between the wearer's eyes and the device. This is one of the reasons why old HMDs were called VR goggles. Late 20th century VR prototypes can be adjusted, so its lenses can match the distance between the device and the user's eyes.

In today's HMDs, lenses focus and reshape images in each eye to create a stereoscopic 3D image. This is perfected by angling two 2D images for each eye which views the world around us differently. By closing one eye, you'll notice how differently the other open eye, views the scene in front of you. You can check out with the other eye as well.

Aside from stereoscopic 3D images, VR headsets increase immersion by widening its user's field of view. This is why majority of VR app and devices today offer 360-degree displays.

To make images and videos more convincing, higher frame rate is incorporated into HMDs. The minimum accepted rate is 60 frames per second (fps). However, top of the line VR headsets today feature 90 to 120 fps.

Bullard Sanford
Memorial Library
120 W Huron Ave. Vassar, MI

## Technologies

### *Head Tracking*

Head tracking is a form of input device. VR systems track how the head moves and adjusts the pictures that are being displayed on the headset. Images shift whenever the user looks from side to side, and up and down.

One of the technologies featured in HMDs is called the six degrees of freedom (6DoF). It plots the head's movement and measures it in terms of x, y, and z axis. The axes are called pitch, yaw and roll which translates to head movements from side to side, and forward and backwards.

Internal components in head tracking systems include a magnetometer, accelerometer, and gyroscope. Some HMDs have LEDs in them to enhance 360-degree views and the pitch, yaw and roll.

Another way to enhance views is HMDs is by minimizing latency or lags. Maximum should be 50 milliseconds. If higher than this, VR headset users will experience lags whenever the head is turned or as virtual sceneries change. This greatly diminishes the quality of VR.

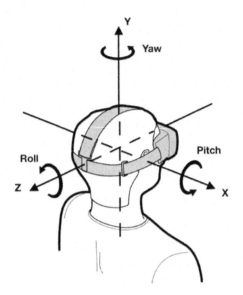

*Head Tracking for Pitch, Yaw and Roll. (c) Oculus*

Head tracking is also equipped with 3D audio. This increases users' sense of immersion. With audio incorporated into head tracking technologies, users can detect changes in the noise around them. Head tracking audio can help them determine if sound is coming from their side, behind, or front. They can also tell whether a sound comes from a distance or just near them.

## *Motion Tracking*

Not all VR headsets have head tracking capabilities though. Mobile HMDs (using smart phones) are not yet equipped with head tracking. Only major players in the field have this feature. They also have motion tracking in their devices.

With motion tracking, users expect to see movements of their hands or arms. Older motion tracking technologies used camera sensors to track hand movements. Recently however, some high-end HMDs have accessories strapped to the headset that uses infrared sensors to detect hand movements.

Other HMDs have a set or wireless controllers that enable users to feel like they're actually using their own hands. Though this technology is yet to be released, it's already making waves in the field.

With this kind of new technology, users can press a button, use thumbsticks, and pull triggers in VR games. Sensors that can detect hand gestures such as waving and pointing can also be found on controllers. Some HMDs have base stations that use lasers to "sweep" an area in order to track its users and detect movement. At times, base stations can track multiple users, a feature especially useful with multi-player VR games.

Other kinds of input devices that has motion tracking capabilities include voice controls treadmills, and smart gloves.

## *Eye Tracking*

With today's advancements in VR, eye tracking is considered the ultimate challenge. It's not yet available on major HMDs, but it is highly anticipated more than the motion tracking capability.

Eye tracking works by detecting eye movements using infrared sensors. It enables a VR game to detect facial reactions from players. It precisely reproduces the reaction of HMD users while looking at a virtual environment or playing games. Its main advantage however, it that it can make depth of field between objects and a user appear more realistic.

VR headsets without eye tracking are in pin-sharp focus, but that's not how humans see the world. Looking at objects from the distance makes objects near the viewer appear blurred. The same thing works when looking at near objects. Objects from afar appear blurry. This is an example of eye tracking technology. HMDs have to be in high-resolution to achieve this kind of feature.

VR developers believe that by incorporating eye tracking into HMDs prevents or lessens simulation sickness. With eye tracking, the brain can match the movement of the eyes with the head.

## *Haptic Interaction*

Basic haptics technology can be found on today's smartphones. This gives you a firsthand idea of this technology.

In VR headsets, a haptics technology works the same way. It provides a force feedback which is a form of reaction caused by a movement in the VR world.

Haptic reaction is usually vibrations experienced by VR users, although many other forms of movement are also part of it. It is caused by a simple touch, or a series of hand movements.

To contribute to the total immersion experience, images, videos and sound are almost always added with haptics.

Aside from smart phones, haptics is often seen and experienced in video games. In other industries, haptics is used in surgery simulation and in-car navigation systems.

# Developing and Creating a VR

Before you can enjoy your cutting-edge HMDs and VR goggles, you need to have a powerful computer that can help you create and view VR videos, and play VR games. You can either buy a VR-ready computer setup or build one for yourself. To help you decide which road to take, here are a few considerations to make:

* VR is expensive. High-end, cutting edge VR devices today headsets costs range from $599 to $799. Computer setups that can run VR cost a minimum of $999. This price though, is only applicable to bundled offers. On the other hand, while prices for VR games and apps differ, they are still higher compared to non-VR ones.

* Having the minimum PC requirements to run VR can provide a good, acceptable VR experience. However, this only works for the first few generations of VR games, videos, and apps. You'll have to up your hardware if you want to play more recent VR games or use new VR apps.

* To provide an easier transition to a VR-ready computer system, the design of your PC should have room for expansion. It should have a bigger CPU with a tool-free access to its interior. At the

same time, it should have options for new configurations that can adapt with VR systems.

* Extra room and space is vital to VR systems. A bigger CPU needs more room. Your CAVE should have ample space as well, so you can move freely in it while playing games.

The reintroduction of virtual reality has sparked a new interest for its use and capabilities. The industries of science and computing technologies, and the businesses that promote VR believe that this re-emerging field can make lots of money sooner than anybody wishes to think.

Greenlight VR, a division of Greenlight Insights however, says otherwise. Greenlight Insights is an industry leader in providing business intelligence for VR and AR companies. According to a 2016 report from Greenlight VR, there is not much interest in paying a lot of money for VR devices among consumers.

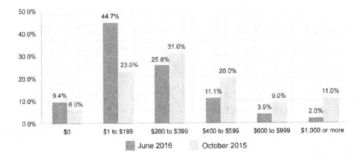

*Consumers are not keen on cashing out on VR devices as seen here in a Greenlight VR report. (c) Greenlight VR via Venture Beat*

If you agree with them, then knowing how to develop and create a VR device, VR videos, and a VR-ready computer can help a big deal. On the contrary, if you have the money to buy VR equipment and create VR videos with them, the next sections can help you decide which ones to buy and use.

Here's everything you need to know about developing and creating VR videos and a VR-ready computer.

### *Building a VR-Ready PC from Scratch*

Building a VR-ready PC from scratch is one way of saving money. It also ensures VR users that they get the features and parts they need and want. If you want to build a PC ready for running VR, your old computer system should be up to date. Old systems just won't do.

According to CNET, a website dedicated to computer technology reviews, you should pick components that will make your PC ready for the onslaught of high-resolution, demanding VR videos and games. Here's a table of their recommendations, as compiled by experts in the field:

| Part | Basic | Mini | All-Power |
|------|-------|------|-----------|
| CPU | Core i5-4590 | Core i5 4690K | Core i7 6700K |
| GPU | AMD Radeon RX 480 | Asus Mini GTX 970 | 2x GTX 980 Ti |
| RAM | 8GB DDR3 | 16GB DDR3 | G.Skill Ripjaws V Series, DDR4 3200, 16GB (1x 16GB) |
| CPU Cooler | Stock | Corsair H60 | Corsair H90 |
| PSU | 550W Corsair CX550M | Silverstone ST45SF-G | SeaSonic Platinum-1200 |
| Motherboard | ASRock H97 Pro4 | Gigabyte GA-Z97N-WiFi | Gigabyte G1 Gaming GA-Z170X-Gaming 7 |
| Storage 1 | Samsung 850 EVO 250GB | Samsung 850 EVO 250GB | Samsung 850 EVO 500GB |
| Storage 2 | None | WD Black 2TB, 7200RPM | WD Black 2TB, 7200RPM |
| OS | Windows 10 Home | Windows 10 Home | Windows 10 Home |

There are three options in this guide table. For each option, only the major PC components are included.

1  *The basic option features recommended hardware and operating system for computers that can run current and recent VR videos, games, and apps.*

2  *The second option enables VR users to build a VR-ready PC that is compact in size, and yet powerful enough to support current VR games and videos.*

3  *The all-power option enables users to build a PC that can support VR games and videos that may be released in the next few years.*

If you want to try out VR just to see what's it all about, CNET recommends that the bare minimum would do just fine.

If you want to head on and buy a ready-made PC system, here's what you can buy.

## *Buying Your VR-Ready Computer System*

If you want to enjoy the total VR immersion, make sure to buy a PC with the specs mentioned above. Unfortunately, even high-end laptops available today are not enough to run VR videos and games. However, if you combine a gaming laptop with your basic VR-ready PC, that could work.

The minimum cost of a VR-ready PC is $999. However, a really good setup could cost around $2,000. For a high-end VR PC, the cost could reach up to $4,000 and more. Before you fork out any money, here's what CNET recommends (arranged from the most affordable to the most expensive one). In this list, PCs with minimum specs required to run VR is presented first, followed by highly specialized setups for VR developers' use.

## Dell XPS 8900 SE

Oculus-ready

$1,199, but there's a $200 discount. You can get it for $999 only if you buy it bundled with an Oculus VR headset.

## Alienware X51 (Mini)

$1,199, but once bundled with Oculus, it also offers a $200 discount.

It has nearly the same hardware configuration with Dell XPS 8900. As the usual with mini PCs however, upgrades for this one is limited.

## Origin PC Chronos

$1,799

To keep the price affordable, the manufacturer used a GeForce 970 graphics card for this set.

## Lenovo Ideacentre Y900

$1,999

This PC features an all-power setup. It has the Core i7 CPU and Nvidia GeForce 980 graphics card.

## Acer Predator G6

$1,999

Has a software overclocking feature for its CPU. A big red "turbo" button on the chassis, once pushed, activates the feature.

## AVADirect Avatar

$2,549

This is arguably the PC that has the most futuristic-looking appearance. It's bulky, too. You'd better prepare a space for this one.

## Velocity Micro Raptor Z55

$2,799

Features the Nvidia 980ti graphics card and a VR-ready front panel which allows easy access to the USB and HDMI ports needed to connect a VR headset.

## Origin PC Eon17-SLX (Laptop)

$3,400

This is actually a bulky laptop. It's only the one of its kind that can run VR and one of the fastest setup in this list. It features a Core i7 processor and a desktop version of the Nvidia980 graphics card.

## Falcon Northwest Tiki

$4,900

The most expensive and fastest VR-ready PC available. Not only can it run VR, it can also be used to create VR videos and games. It has a very high-end setup and a massive 6TB of storage.

To help you decide which one to buy, or if the one you're eyeing is not on this list, make sure to get a setup that can maintain a steady fps per eye (see Physical Components above). The minimum is 60fps, but going for 90fps is way better.

Investing in a higher hardware setup and system configuration can help you experience a smoother VR. It can also help you prepare for more intense VR games, videos and apps in the future. You can also personalize your setup with faster graphics card, more memory and storage, plus ergonomically-designed mouse and keyboard. Any of the setups discussed here anyway are highly customizable.

Note also that PCs can fluctuate in price if you want them built to order. At the same time, availability and prices can change, sometimes even on a weekly basis.

## Creating VR Videos

With a PC ready to run VR, you can now create your own videos. You can always buy a VR game, but you can create your own videos.

Video games have already been showcasing realistic 3D computer-generated worlds for years. Capturing 360-degree videos of real life locations for your own use however, is new. You have to know and understand how to do it and the necessary equipment you have to get.

Here's how to film videos that's fed into your VR headset and the equipment you'll need.

### *The Equipment*

You have three options when choosing the right equipment. You can either create a camera rig, buy a VR-ready rig, or buy a 360-degree video camera.

If you want to create your own VR-ready camera rig, you'll need several action cameras setup in a single rig. You must prepare a camera rig and 6-10 digital action cameras. The cameras should be attached in a spherical shape. This eliminates any gaps in the VR video that will be taken shortly. The cameras are specifically mounted in this way because the designated specific angle for each camera enables it to capture overlapping field of view.

Alternatively, you can buy a camera rig. You can just simply attach your action cameras (and how many microphones you want) onto the rig and you're ready to go.

If you're willing to allot a considerable sum for your VR equipment, you can also buy a VR-ready camera rig. It's expensive and is intended for professional use. If you want to try it out, a list of top camera rigs can be seen below.

Now, your best bet would be to purchase a camera with 360-degree capability instead. It's cheaper and easier to use.

| Top Camera Rigs | Top Action Cameras | Top VR-Ready Camera Rigs | Top 360-degree Video Cameras |
|---|---|---|---|
| 1. 360RIZE Pro7 v2 360° Plug-n-Play Holder $455 | 1. GoPro Hero4 Black $499.99 | 1. GoPro Odyssey $15k | 1. Ricoh Theta S $350 |
| 2. Freedom360 F360 Broadcaster Mount $575 | 2. GoPro Hero4 Silver $282.75 | 2. MoooVr $12.5k | 2. 360Fly 4K $500 |
| 3. MaxxMove 360° Six-Camera Mount $290 | 3. GoPro Hero4 White $269.99 | 3. Lytro Immerge (not for sale in the consumer market. Alternative: Light Field $210 or Illum $299.99) | 3. Giroptic 360cam $500 |
| 4. Kolor Abyss Underwater 360 Rig $5,450 | 4. GoPro Hero Session $299.99 | 4. Facebook Surround 360 (Open-source. Downloadable manual found | 4. VSN Mobil V.360-degree Action Cam $499 |
| 5. GoPro Omni (Rig Only) | 5. Kodak PixPro SP1 $177.80 | | 5. ALLie Camera $499 |
| | | | 6. Kodak PixPro SP360 4K Action |

Whatever your choice is, here's a detailed list of top cameras and rig that you can choose from:

| | | | |
|---|---|---|---|
| $1,500 | 6. Polaroid Cube $98.15 | here: GitHub.) | Cam $499 |
| 6. Selens SE-GPP6WP Virtual Reality Spherical Panorama Frame Mount $570 | 7. Drift HD Ghost-S $267 | 5. Videostich Orah 4i $3.6k | 7. LG 360 Cam $200 |
| | 8. GoPro Hero+ $139.99 | 6. GoPro Omni $5k | 8. Nikon KeyMission 360 $499 |
| 7. Entaniya Fisheye Rig for Three $430 | 9. Kodak Pixpro SP360 4K $499 | 7. Nokia OZO $60k | |
| | 10. Sony POV Action Camera (HDR-AS100V) $299.99 | 8. Jaunt One $4.5k/day (rent only) | |
| | | 9. Eye Camera $4.5k/week (rent only, but they offer custom rigs at different prices) | |

## *Field of Vision*

In VR, field of vision (FOV) is the extent, size and coverage of an observable environment. Because of this, shooting a VR video is nothing like shooting a regular video.

FOV in VR is 360 degrees in order to totally immerse the VR user. This means that the observable environment should be shot in its entirety. In fact, using a VR rig can capture even the filming crew. In your case, your VR rig or VR camera will eventually capture you as well. Everything around you and the camera will actually be captured.

It's both limiting and liberating when shooting a VR video. You have to be creative considering you'll be included in the shot. You can practice your filming skills. However, you have to make a way to hide or keep yourself from being seen in the videos if you don't want to be included in the shots.

It would help if you take the time to scout your location first before you shoot videos. Take the entire space of an area into consideration. Envision your video, make sure there's enough lighting, and be creative with your placement of your camera (or cameras).

## Camera Location

Consider the role of the person shooting the video. This helps capture the action of the scene. This means that the location of the camera depends whether the VR user wearing the headset is a participant or an observer in the video.

On the other hand, whatever the role of the VR user is, it's important to place the camera around or in the center of the activity. Doing so enables the viewer to explore the scene, seeing all the interesting details in the video from all directions. Imagine Google Map's Streetview. Remember, camera placement is important to get your story across.

## Camera Movement

It's important to calculate the motion of a VR video first before shooting it. Haphazard VR video shooting can cause nausea on the viewer's part and can eventually disconnect them from the experience.

Still, camera movement is needed if the video aims for action. This depends on the purpose of the video. If you want a simple virtual scene, there's not much movement needed there. If you're shooting a moving car, that's whole different kind of story.

Movement of the camera will depend entirely on its holder. For example, to shoot the moving car and the environment around it, the camera holder should be moving as well. Being in another car, chasing after the car being shot in the video can help. Using a drone or camera track can also be useful.

However, as mentioned earlier, the one holding the camera will be included in the video. You can use a software program to blend the camera holder in the video to the surrounding environment. This is part of the post-production process.

### *Post-Production Process*

After shooting the 360° video, there is still so much to be done. All the footage and shots will be downloaded and synchronized. After that, they will have to be "stitched" together to form the whole video.

Now you have to put your shots together. For this, you'll need a VR software or app.

### Creating VR Content

VR apps and software enable users to create VR content easily. Here are the top VR content apps that you can use after you've captured your VR videos.

## *For Smartphones*

## Photo Sphere

Photo Sphere is a VR app that runs on both iOS and Android smart phones. It's a free app that comes with Google's Street View app. It's one of the best because you can easily shoot videos and create a VR video out the pictures that you've taken. An onscreen guide will help you through the process if you're new to the app or if you're not familiar on how to create VR videos.

Because you'll be using just your smartphone, it'll be hard to capture the images at first though. You'll have to make a few rotations to get the whole picture in your video. However, the app can perfectly stitch them together.

You can also share the VR videos that you capture through Google Maps.

## 360 Panorama

360 Panorama is available for $1.99 and it can be used on iOS. It's easy to use with your iPhone camera. It works the same way with Google's Photo Sphere. You capture the images with your phone and the 360 Panorama app will stitch it together to create a 360-degree video. Unlike Photo Sphere however, you don't have to take several rotations in order to take a 360-degree

video. It's quick to use and it provides more options for sharing your VR videos.

**Panorama 360**

Like Photo Sphere, Panorama 360 is available for free. It can be downloaded from Google Play Store. Aside from providing the same functions as other VR apps have, it also has additional features. You can add effects and filters to your videos with this app. It's also compatible with Google's basic VR headset, the Google Cardboard.

**Splash**

Splash is also available for free, though it can be downloaded for iOS phones. It's also easy to use with its simple interface. It also features integration with social networks for quick sharing. It's also compatible with Google Cardboard.

On the other hand, VR apps are not always perfect. It takes time to get used to them. However, they are a good start if you want to move on to sphere cameras and VR camera rigs.

### *For Desktops*

You can move on to desktop-based VR software if you've decided to use VR cameras or rigs. Some of them come with software of their own, but the ones in this list are the most commonly used and are the top ones among the rest, too.

### Unreal Engine

Unreal Engine is available for free. It's a game engine that enables users to create VR games and videos. It more popular with game developers though.

If you're aiming for VR videos, Unreal Engine can help you create cinematic-like type ones. The visual effects are stunning, and the lighting is dynamic and advanced.

Moreover, Unreal Engine allows users to create VR from 2D images and videos.

### Unity 3D

Unity 3D is also available for free. It's a 3D engine that is easy enough for beginners to use, but still powerful for developers.

Unity 3D can be used to create VR games, videos, and apps. It's a cross-platform engine that enables users to develop their VR for use in smartphones, desktops, or game consoles.

## CryEngine VR First

Cryengine's VR First is a game engine. It can be used for free, but additional features and support become available once you become a member. Crytek, the German software company that developed Cryengine, also offers enterprise licensing for companies.

Cryengine is cross-platform. VR videos and games it can produce can be played or viewed in Oculus Rift, Xbox One, Windows PC, Sony PlayStation 4, and Linux PC.

## Lumberyard

Lumberyard is a 3D game engine that comes free with Amazon Web Services (AWS). It is available for free.

Lumberyard enables it users to create high-quality VR games, share them, and store them via AWS Cloud. It's also connected with Twitch, a top community for video gamers.

-------

Now you're ready to get yourself an HMD or VR device.

# Chapter 3 - VR Trends

Here are five of the best VR devices available today. You can choose from a cheap headset that works with smartphones to ones that are expensive. All these headsets require VR software and a powerful computer in order to enable users to create VR videos and games. Specifications and price for each device are shown below. Whichever you choose, here's the best options.

## Google Cardboard

Let's start with Google's Cardboard. It's the simplest and cheapest VR available today. It's a folded cardboard turned VR headset. You can download the kit and manual for free from the Google Play store. You can even download its template from elsewhere in the Internet.

However, if you want other models, you can buy a kit for as low as $9. The most expensive kits can go as high as $85. That's still cheap compared to what you'll discover later with other headsets.

Meanwhile, if you think Google is playing it safe amidst the heavy VR battle that's raging between Facebook's Oculus and HTC's Vive. You're wrong. Google has the Daydream, but let's include the Cardboard because its simplicity and affordable price has the potential to enable users from all walks of life to experience VR. Remember, VR is expensive. Google however, has made a way for all of us to get a glimpse of VR and enjoy it.

What's more, there are hundreds of VR apps available in Google Play. Cardboard users can enjoy their simple VR headsets because of the numerous sources of VR games to play and VR videos to watch.

*Google Cardboard is literally cut and folded cardboard turned into a VR headset. (c) Google*

Here's how you can enjoy Google Cardboard:

*Download the free kit and manual from Google VR, or you can buy viewers from various online vendors*

*If you got the free kit, follow the instructions to build the VR headset*

*Download the Google Cardboard app on your smartphone and configure your phone with the app*

*Put your phone in the slot in the headset*

*Use the Cardboard and enjoy!*

# Sony PlayStation VR

The price ranges from $399 to $399.99 and here are its basic specifications:

| | |
|---|---|
| Headset Type: | Tethered |
| Connections: | HDMI, USB 2.0 |
| Resolution: | 960 x 1080 (per eye) |
| FOV: | 100 degrees |
| Refresh Rate: | 120Hz |
| Controls: | PlayStation Move, DualShock 4 |
| Sensors: | Motion, external visual positioning |
| Hardware: | PlayStation 4 |
| Software: | PlayStation 4 |

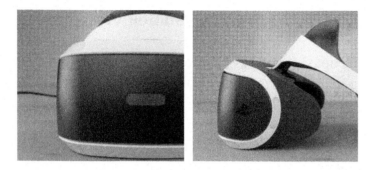

The Sony PlayStation VR front and side views.
(c) Sony PlayStation via PC Magazine

For interested buyers, here are some of the top games that can be played on Sony PS4 VR:

| | |
|---|---|
| Eve: Valkyrie | a multiplayer shooter game from Icelandic developer CCP Games |
| Thumper | a rhythm violence game from game developer Drool |
| Until Dawn: Rush of Blood | a arcade shooter horror game by Supermassive Games |
| Battlezone | a VR remake of a classic game of Battlezone, a first-person shooter arcade game from Acitivision. Original game was developed by Atari |
| Rez Infinite | a rail shooter music video game from Sega |
| Job Simulator | VR simulation video game from Owlchemy Labs |
| Batman Arkham VR | an action-adventure video game based on DC Comics' Batman |
| Wayward Sky | an action VR video game by Uber Entertainment |

Sony's VR headset is considerably new. It was only released at the start of fall in 2016. It's affordable and provides good quality graphics. It's a good addition to the PlayStation 4 console and it doesn't require a powerful PC to run. What's more, Sony's game console has hundreds of games available. This ensures that this headset's users will surely enjoy using this one.

However, there are a few problems with it. It's not properly sealing out all the light once you've worn it. Its motion tracking is lagging at times, which is highly questionable considering it has one of the highest refresher rates among the headsets listed here.

It's also notable that its accessories are not included in the price mentioned above. It's not even included in the package. You have to buy them separately. If PlayStation VR has to perform its best, it should have the PS4 camera and Move controllers. Unfortunately, you have to buy them separately.

Still, PS4 VR can provide high-quality VR cinematic experience once on its Theater Mode. While it performs well with VR games, it can be used to watch VR movies and videos on a wide screen.

## HTC Vive

HTC Vive and its accessories. (c) HTC/Valve

| | |
|---|---|
| Price: | $799-799.99 |
| Headset Type: | Tethered |
| Connections: | HDMI, DisplayPort, USB 2.0, USB 3.0 |
| Resolution: | 1080 x 1200 (per eye) |
| FOV: | 110 degrees |
| Refresh Rate: | 90Hz |
| Controls: | HTC Vive motion controllers |

| Sensors: | Motion, camera, external motion tracking |
|---|---|
| Hardware: | PC |
| Software: | SteamVR |

HTC Vive is a partnership between HTC and Valve Corporation. While HTC is the developer, the owner of the headset's technology is Valve Corp. Initial prototypes have been used in demonstrations as early as 2013. However, it wasn't until 2016 that the device became available to the public.

HTC Vive is currently the best VR headset there is. It's been consecutively receiving good reviews from the experts. It enables its users to experience simple VR moves from walking around a room, to more complex VR moves like grabbing an object in a VR environment.

With this headset, users are tethered to a powerful gaming computer while numerous cables are plugged in to the VR system. Make room for this one.

Aside from the headset itself, the Vive kit has two base stations and two motion controllers.

Other top VR headsets don't have this feature yet.

To provide users with head tracking that spans 360-degrees, the Vive provides 70 sensors with a high 90Hz refresh rate. This reduces lagging, if not remove it from occurring.

For interested buyers, here are the best games to play on HTC Vive:

| | |
|---|---|
| Fantastic Contraption | an object-building VR video game by Northway Games |
| Job Simulator | also plays on Sony PS4 VR |
| The Lab | a VR video game from Valve Corporation |
| Apollo 11 Experience | an interactive adventure VR game by Immersive VR Education Ltd. |
| Cloudlands: VR Minigolf | from game developer Cloudhead Games |
| The Gallery Episode 1: Call of the Starseed | an 80s dark fantasy film-inspired episodic VR game also by Cloudhead Games |
| SculptVR | an indie world building game developed by Nathan Rowe |
| Space Pirate Trainer | a first-person alien shooter VR game by I-Illusions |
| theBlu | a deep-sea exploration game by indie game developer Wevr, Inc. |
| Tilt Brush | a VR painting app from Google |

# Oculus Rift

| | |
|---|---|
| Price: | $599-599.99 |
| Headset Type: | Tethered |
| Connections: | HDMI, USB 2.0, USB 3.0 |
| Resolution: | 1080 x 1200 (per eye) |
| FOV: | 110 degrees |
| Refresh Rate: | 90Hz |
| Controls: | Oculus Touch, Xbox One gamepad |
| Sensors: | Motion, external visual positioning |
| Hardware: | PC |
| Software: | Oculus |

The Oculus Rift (c) Facebook Inc. via Wareable

The Oculus Rift has a long history.

Oculus was originally developed by Oculus VR, a startup company headed by Palmer Luckey. He is 24 years old now, but he was only 20 when the company started in 2012. Two years later in 2014, Mark Zuckerberg of Facebook Inc. bought the company for $2 billion because of its apparent success. Luckey was only 22. He's one of the richest American entrepreneurs under 40YO today, as mentioned in Forbes magazine.

The Oculus Rift is better than Sony's PS4 VR. On the other hand, it is not as good as HTC Vive, but it offers a better immersion experience compared to Google Cardboard and the other mobile headsets you'll see later on. However, it is still more popular than HTC Vive.

With Oculus, you can view VR objects up close because it can track your head's movement. You can lean in at objects to get a closer look. However, you need to have a powerful computer to use this headset.

Here's a list of the top games and apps you can play on the Rift:

| | |
|---|---|
| Eve: Valkyrie | also plays on Sony PS4 VR |
| Darknet | a VR cyberpunk hacking game by indie game designer E McNeill |
| Chronos | an adventure role-playing game (RPG) from game developer Gunfire Games |
| Keep Talking and Nobody Explodes | by 505 Games |
| Adrift | from game developer Carbon Games |
| AirMech: Command | a strategic multi-player arena game also by Carbon Games |
| BlazeRush | a combat racing game from Russian game studio Targem Games |
| Virtual Desktop | a VR app that enables users to hook up their VR headsets easily to their PCs. App is developed by Crytek |
| The Climb | also from Crytek, is a VR exploration game |
| Damaged Core | by High Voltage Software, it is a first-person shooter game |
| Edge of Nowhere | a 3rd-person action adventure game from Insomniac Games |
| Lucky's Tale | an adventure game from game developer Playful |

# Samsung Gear VR

| | |
|---|---|
| Price: | $99-99.50 SRP |
| Headset Type: | Mobile |
| Connections: | USB 2.0, USB 3.0 |
| Resolution: | 2560 x 1440 |
| Controls: | Onboard touchpad, Bluetooth controllers |
| Sensors: | Motion, presence |
| Hardware: | Android |
| Software: | Samsung Gear VR powered by Oculus |

Samsung Gear VR (c) Samsung via Wareable

Like Google Cardboard, Samsung Gear VR is mobile-based. A smartphone has to be inserted in a slot allotted for it inside the headset. The quality of VR videos and games viewed through this headset depends on the type of smartphone used in it.

However, no matter what Samsung smartphone is used in it, its widened angle and darkened tint still makes it a better headset than the mobile-based Google Cardboard.

Here are some of the best apps and games users can play and run in Gear VR:

| | |
|---|---|
| Anshar Wars 2 | a dog-fighting space combat game by OZWE |
| Netflix | the popular movie website |
| Gunjack | a stationary arcade shooter game by CCP Games |
| Land's End | by UsTwo Games, it is a puzzle journey game |
| Oculus Arcade | setup in a literal arcade game shop, this beta version features limited play arcade games from Sega, Bandai, Namco, etc. The Oculus Arcade is of course, developed by Oculus |
| Bazaar | an adventure exploration game from Temple Gate Games |
| Esper 2 | a puzzle narrative VR game By Coatsink Software |

## Bonus: Google Daydream View

Google Daydream is Google's newest VR headset. It's a step up from their first generation Cardboard. As another mobile-based VR headset, it's lighter than Samsung Gear VR.

Google has also released Google Pixel and Pixe XL, smartphones that are compatible with Daydream View. Other smartphone developers are expected to create Daydream View-compatible phones in the near future. They all expect this latest device from Google to provide a high-quality VR mobile experience.

Introductory price is $79. Its resolution depends on the smartphone that the user will use, unlike Gear VR which has a fixed resolution of 2560x1440. It has a motion sensor and a handheld remote for controls. The device runs on an Android 7.0 Nougat software platform.

Google Daydream View (c) Google

Other notable VR headsets available in the market today:

| | | |
|---|---|---|
| | Carl Zeiss VR One Plus<br><br>*Image source: Carl Zeiss via TechRadar* | $129* |
| | Microsoft HoloLens - combines VR and AR<br><br>*Image source: Microsoft via Wareable* | $3,000* |
| | Razer OSVR HDK 2<br><br>*Image source: Razer via Wareable* | $399* |
| | Fove VR<br>*Image source: Razer via Wareable* | $599* |

| | | |
|---|---|---|
| | LG 360 VR<br><br>*Image source: LG via Road to VR* | $169.99 – $199.99* |
| | Homido<br><br>*Image source: Homido* | $60-75* |
| | Carl Zeiss VR One GX<br><br>- Like VR One, but without the headstrap like Google Cardboard<br><br>*Image source: Carl Zeiss via Pocket Link* | $120* |

*suggested retail price (SRP)

71

Microsoft has also partnered with other leading manufacturers of computing products with the aim of create Windows-based VR headsets. For the next years, the public will be seeing a variety of VR headsets including ones from Lenovo, HP, Dell, Asus, and Acer. According to Microsoft, they are aiming to release products with a starting price of $299.

With this kind of news, it looks like the future of VR is set to soar high.

# Chapter 4 – VR And Beyond!

Virtual reality has been around for decades. However, its re-invention and re-introduction has opened up many possibilities for many industries including:

*Healthcare and medicine*

*Military*

*Architecture*

*Art and entertainment*

*Education*

*Business*

*Media and communications*

*Sport*

*Fashion*

*Rehabilitation and therapy*

The list of applications in various industries for VR is endless.

The biggest beneficiary is the field of medicine. Development in surgery simulation has enabled doctors to effectively show students how certain surgical techniques are performed. This is all done using a virtual patient.

A video feed of a recent surgery in Europe has been shown to students through a VR headset. VR has truly become an effective training aid for doctors and medicine students.

Patients can also be diagnosed through VR examination. A virtual representation of the human body enables doctors to see in detail its different internal parts. It is a better way of looking at patients compared to MRIs, CT-scans, and x-rays.

The aviation industry has also benefited largely from VR. Three-dimensional simulations have been used to train pilots, especially in the military.

In the commercial aviation industry, VR is used to simulate new aircrafts. This way, aircraft manufacturers spend less money and time compared to building a prototype and testing it beforehand.

Unfortunately, despite its popular use, many people are still not aware of the resurgence of VR.

According to a report by SuperData, a leading games market intelligence provider, 52% of consumers have no knowledge whatsoever about VR and other technologies related to it. Worse, the same percentage is applied to uninterested people.

Despite this, the VR industry is booming.

## 2016+ Verdict

2016 is the year of virtual reality for a reason. Not because many high-end VR devices are released for this year, but because its market potential reaches a wide audience.

Google for example, has proven once again that technology is for everybody. According to a 2016 report by the Financial Times, Google's Cardboard headset has reached the most consumers in worldwide market. Cheap and low-end as it is, proved to be an advantage.

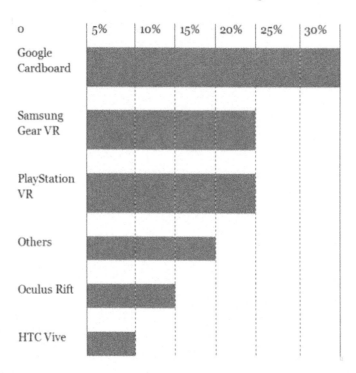

The Financial Times reports VR headset share worldwide with Google Cardboard as the leader.

New VR products were announced to be released starting from 2012. Since then, the VR industry has been predicted to reach the $3 billion mark for 2016. Here are the reasons why.

**Video Games**

After the announcement of various computer and technology companies to release VR headsets in 2012, many game developers started creating their VR-based video games. By the time that Oculus Rift and HTC Vive released their products, there were already games and apps that can be played in them.

This move proved to be influential in raising the interest in the VR market. SuperData estimated that as 2016 ends, the video gaming industry focused on VR will have reached $5.1 billion with Europe as its biggest market.

VIRTUAL REALITY GAMING REGIONAL MARKET SIZE 2016E

North America
$1.5B

Europe
$1.9B

Asia
$1.1B

Rest of World
$0.6B

Mobile in Asia is the first step toward Virtual Reality's $12.3B 2021E industry. Asia will account for more than half of worldwide mobile VR users next year, helping it quickly gain a quarter of the global market. Mobile's accessible barrier to entry will lead to PC and console users to jump on board in North America and Europe, leading the industry to earn $5.1B in 2016E. As hardware and software developers respond to expanding consumer demand, this market will grow from 2016 to 2019E by a CAGR of 16.9%.

$5.1B
Total worldwide market for the Virtual Reality gaming hardware, software and peripherals market, 2016E

Mobile    PC    Console

$12.3B
$8.9B
$5.1B
$660M

2015    2016E    2017E    2018E

VR market reaches $5.1 billion for 2016 as seen here in a report by SuperData, a leading market research firm focused on the gaming and VR industry. (c) SuperData

Based on the report, $1 billion of the sales come from mobile users, while $3.5 billion from PC-based users, and $650 million from console gamers.

## Media and Communications

The New York Times, a leading print and online newspaper in the US, has released a VR app that allows their readers to view news as if they were actually there. The release came as a surprise. Apparently, VR can be used as a tool for delivering news.

With more and more people becoming active online, showcasing VR's capabilities to deliver news is set to spark added interest in VR devices. The release of Google's Cardboard has also complimented the release of VR apps. News can be viewed via smartphones, which is the main source of videos and apps used in the Cardboard.

## Travel and Tourism

VR now enables travelers to visit a street in the city or country that they want to visit. The tourism industry wants to take advantage of this kind of experience. Agencies can promote their travel packages using VR with a 360-degree view of famous sites in various places around the world.

## Consumer Retail

The next big thing in the shopping experience is VR. Soon, shoppers can see and feel the products they want to buy even if they are not physically present in the stores.

The healthcare and aviation industries were the first takers when VR seemed to have ceased to exist to the world. However, the videogame, software, tourism, consumer retail, and media industries have also tapped into the VR world and want a piece of the pie.

# The Next Big Thing

The future of VR is still uncertain. Market analysis has shown different forecasts since VR started to show its revenue potential.

According to a 2016 report by Goldman Sachs (a leading investment banking company in the US), the VR industry is set to balloon to $80 billion by 2025.

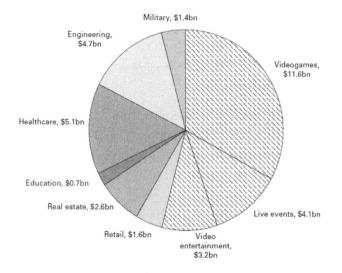

VR and AR use by assumption for 2025. (c) Goldman Sachs via Bloomberg

According to the report, the software sector of the VR industry will reach $35 billion, while VR devices industry will reach 45 $billion. The $80 billion sales figure is expected to come from the following:

Video games - $11.6B, 216M estimated users

Healthcare - $5.1B, 3.1M estimated users

Engineering - $4.7B, 3.2M estimated users

Live events - $4.1B, 91M estimated users

Video entertainment - $3.2B, 72M estimated users

Real estate - $2.6B, 0.3M estimated users

Retail - $1.6B, 32M estimated users

Military - $1.4B, 0.7M estimated users

Education - $0.7B, 15M estimated users

Meanwhile, SuperData has revealed their own report. By 2020, they predict that the VR industry will have gained $40 billion in sales.

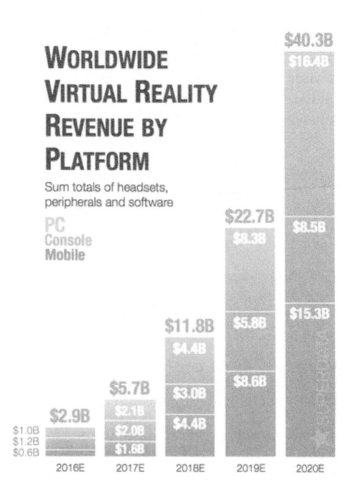

WORLDWIDE VIRTUAL REALITY REVENUE BY PLATFORM

Sum totals of headsets, peripherals and software

PC
Console
Mobile

| | 2016E | 2017E | 2018E | 2019E | 2020E |
|---|---|---|---|---|---|

$2.9B
$1.0B
$1.2B
$0.6B

$5.7B
$2.1B
$2.0B
$1.6B

$11.8B
$4.4B
$3.0B
$4.4B

$22.7B
$8.3B
$5.8B
$8.6B

$40.3B
$16.4B
$8.5B
$15.3B

SuperData predicts VR industry to reach $40 billion sales by 2020. (c) SuperData

Whatever the forecasts are, one this is for sure. Virtual reality will become big just a few years from 2016.

# Conclusion

Unfortunately, medical researchers are worried what VR might do to users' health. We are all sailing through unchartered waters.

Oculus for example, includes precautions in the sale of their kits. They warn users that prolonged use can lead to eye-strain and problems with eye and hand coordination. We're literally tricking our brains and as a result, the body is following suit.

This is just one problem that scientists believe will be hard to combat because VR is fairly new. They can't quantify the results nearly enough to come up with solid conclusions and solutions.

Still, VR is viewed as the next big platform in the computer world.

For this to truly take its shape, VR developers and manufacturers should improve user experience, provide more content, and bring prices of devices down. Virtual reality can be as ever-present as the smartphone, should these happen.

Thank you again for purchasing this book!

CPSIA information can be obtained
at www.ICGtesting.com
Printed in the USA
BVOW06s1828211216
471539BV00017B/160/P